The New Imperial Edition
BASS SONGS

Set of 2 Accompaniment CDs

Compiled, Edited and Arranged by
SYDNEY NORTHCOTE

BASS SONGS

This set of Accompaniment CDs matches the Boosey & Hawkes music collection of the same title, HL48008371   ISMN: M-051-90450-1

BOOSEY & HAWKES

DISTRIBUTED BY

HAL•LEONARD®
CORPORATION
7777 W. BLUEMOUND RD. P.O. BOX 13819 MILWAUKEE, WI 53213

www.boosey.com
www.halleonard.com

ORIGINAL FOREWORD

THE NEW IMPERIAL EDITION OF SOLO SONGS has been designed as a chronological anthology of song from the Lutenists down to the present day. As other albums will be devoted exclusively to operatic and oratorio arias these are generally omitted from the present volumes.

Manifestly, the selection must be indicative rather than comprehensive or merely exclusive and is essentially practical, not personal. Each song is briefly annotated and, except where indicated, appears in the original key or is set for the voice which it is normally associated.

Apart from obvious restrictions, the choice has been largely determined by certain positive needs. To provide the singing teacher and student alike with a working catalogue as a basis for more specialized research into the varied treasures of the literature of song; to give to festival committees and examination bodies a ready way of governing without unduly restricting the dangerous freedom of choice classes; to present the would-be accompanist with a convenient means of studying the many-sided aspects of his exacting technique; and, lastly, to offer to all singers, whether amateur or professional, a practical and logical conspectus of the diversities of lyrical song over a period of some three hundred years. If, in addition these books will do something to combat the present-day weakness for vocal exhibitionism or narrow eclecticism the labour of their preparation will be doubly justified.

Croydon 1949   **SYDNEY NORTHCOTE**

DISC TWO Track List

	TITLE	COMPOSER
1	The Lime Tree (Der Lindenbaum)	Franz Schubert
2	Love leads to battle (Pupille nere)	Giovanni Buononcini
3	Love that's true will live forever (Si, trai ceppi)	George Frideric Handel
4	Money, O!	Michael Head
5	My Lagan Love	arr. Hamilton Harty
6	My Last Abode (Aufenthalt)	Franz Schubert
7	The Owl Is Abroad	Henry Purcell
8	The Self-Banished	John Blow
9	The Solitary One (Der Einsame)	Richard Strauss
10	The Song of the Flea	Ludwig van Beethoven
11	Thoughts at Eventide (Abendempfindung)	Wolfgang Amadeus Mozart
12	Tobacco	Tobias Hume
13	To the Forest	Piotr Ilyich Tschaikowsky
14	The Two Grenadiers (Die beiden Grenadiere)	Robert Schumann
15	The Valley (Le Vallon)	Charles Gounod

Pianist on the recording: Laura Ward

COMPOSER INDEX

	DISC ONE	DISC TWO
LULLY, JEAN BAPTISTE		
All your shades (Bois épais)	[1]	
MENDELSSOHN, FELIX		
I am a roamer	[11]	
MOZART, WOLFGANG AMADEUS		
Thoughts at Eventide (Abendempfindung)		[11]
PURCELL, HENRY		
Arise, ye subterranean winds (Tempest)	[2]	
Hear! ye Gods of Britain	[10]	
The Owl Is Abroad		[7]
RACHMANINOFF, SERGEI		
By the Grave (Sur la tombe encore fraîche)	[4]	
SCHUBERT, FRANZ		
The Lay of the Imprisoned Huntsman	[15]	
(Lied des gefangenen Jägers)		
The Lime Tree (Der Lindenbaum)		[1]
My Last Abode (Aufenthalt)		[6]
SCHUMANN, ROBERT		
The Last Toast	[14]	
(Auf das Trinkglas eines verstorbenen Freundes)		
The Two Grenadiers (Die beiden Grenadiere)		[14]
STRAUSS, RICHARD		
The Solitary One (Der Einsame)		[9]
TRADITIONAL GERMAN TRINKLIED		
Drinking	[6]	
TSCHAIKOWSKY, PIOTR ILYICH		
To the Forest		[13]
WOOD, CHARLES		
Ethiopia Saluting the Colours	[9]	

ORIGINAL FOREWORD

THE NEW IMPERIAL EDITION OF SOLO SONGS has been designed as a chronological anthology of song from the Lutenists down to the present day. As other albums will be devoted exclusively to operatic and oratorio arias these are generally omitted from the present volumes.

Manifestly, the selection must be indicative rather than comprehensive or merely exclusive and is essentially practical, not personal. Each song is briefly annotated and, except where indicated, appears in the original key or is set for the voice which it is normally associated.

Apart from obvious restrictions, the choice has been largely determined by certain positive needs. To provide the singing teacher and student alike with a working catalogue as a basis for more specialized research into the varied treasures of the literature of song; to give to festival committees and examination bodies a ready way of governing without unduly restricting the dangerous freedom of choice classes; to present the would-be accompanist with a convenient means of studying the many-sided aspects of his exacting technique; and, lastly, to offer to all singers, whether amateur or professional, a practical and logical conspectus of the diversities of lyrical song over a period of some three hundred years. If, in addition these books will do something to combat the present-day weakness for vocal exhibitionism or narrow eclecticism the labour of their preparation will be doubly justified.

Croydon 1949   **SYDNEY NORTHCOTE**

ABOUT THE ENHANCED CD

In addition to piano accompaniments playable on both your CD player and computer, this enhanced CD also includes tempo adjustment and transposition software for CD-ROM computer use only. This software, known as Amazing Slow Downer, was originally created for use in pop music to allow singers and players the freedom to independently adjust both tempo and pitch elements. Because we believe there may be valuable educational use for these features in classical and theatre music, we have included this software as a tool for both the teacher and student. For quick and easy installation instructions of this software, please see below.

In recording a piano accompaniment we necessarily must choose one tempo. Our choice of tempo, phrasing, *ritardandos*, and dynamics is carefully considered. But by the nature of recording, it is only one choice.

However, we encourage you to explore your own interpretive ideas, which may differ from our recordings. This new software feature allows you to adjust the tempo up and down without affecting the pitch. Likewise, Amazing Slow Downer allows you to shift pitch up and down without affecting the tempo. We recommend that these new tempo and pitch adjustment features be used with care and insight. Ideally, you will be using these recorded accompaniments and Amazing Slow Downer for practice only.

The audio quality may be somewhat compromised when played through the Amazing Slow Downer. This compromise in quality will not be a factor in playing the CD audio track on a normal CD player or through another audio computer program.

INSTALLATION INSTRUCTIONS:

For Macintosh OS 8, 9 and X:
• Load the CD-ROM into your CD-ROM Drive on your computer.
• Each computer is set up a little differently. Your computer may automatically open the audio CD portion of this enhanced CD and begin to play it.
• To access the CD-ROM features, double-click on the data portion of the CD-ROM (which will have the Hal Leonard icon in red and be named as the book).
• Double-click on the "Amazing OS 8 (9 or X)" folder.
• Double-click "Amazing Slow Downer"/"Amazing X PA" to run the software from the CD-ROM, or copy this file to your hard disk and run it from there.
• Follow the instructions on-screen to get started. The Amazing Slow Downer should display tempo, pitch and mix bars. Click to select your track and adjust pitch or tempo by sliding the appropriate bar to the left or to the right.

For Windows:
• Load the CD-ROM into your CD-ROM Drive on your computer.
• Each computer is set up a little differently. Your computer may automatically open the audio CD portion of this enhanced CD and begin to play it.
• To access the CD-ROM features, click on My Computer then right click on the Drive that you placed the CD in. Click Open. You should then see a folder named "Amazing Slow Downer". Click to open the "Amazing Slow Downer" folder.
• Double-click "setup.exe" to install the software from the CD-ROM to your hard disk. Follow the on-screen instructions to complete installation.
• Go to "Start," "Programs" and find the "Amazing Slow Downer" folder. Go to that folder and select the "Amazing Slow Downer" software.
• Follow the instructions on-screen to get started. The Amazing Slow Downer should display tempo, pitch and mix bars. Click to select your track and adjust pitch or tempo by sliding the appropriate bar to the left or to the right.
• Note: On Windows NT, 2000 and XP, the user should be logged in as the "Administrator" to guarantee access to the CD-ROM drive. Please see the help file for further information.

MINIMUM SYSTEM REQUIREMENTS:

For Macintosh:
Power Macintosh; Mac OS 8.5 or higher; 4 MB Application RAM; 8x Multi-Session CD-ROM drive

For Windows:
Pentium, Celeron or equivalent processor; Windows 95, 98, ME, NT, 2000, XP; 4 MB Application RAM; 8x Multi-Session CD-ROM drive